Winner of the 2010 Cave Canem Poetry Prize

SELECTED BY ELIZABETH ALEXANDER

Inaugurated in 1999 with Natasha Trethewey's *Domestic Work*, selected by Rita Dove, the **Cave Canem Poetry Prize** is an annual first-book award dedicated to the discovery of exceptional manuscripts by African American poets.

Founded in 1996 by Toi Derricotte and Cornelius Eady, **Cave Canem Foundation** is a home for the many voices of African American poetry and is committed to cultivating the artistic and professional development of African American poets. The organization's community has grown from an initial gathering of 27 poets to become an influential movement with a renowned faculty; a high-achieving fellowship of 302; and programs delivered in New York City, at the University of Pittsburgh (Pittsburgh and Greensburg), and nationally.

www.cavecanempoets.org

SPIT BACK A BOY

POEMS BY IAIN HALEY POLLOCK

SPIT BACK A BOY

THE UNIVERSITY OF GEORGIA PRESS • ATHENS & LONDON

Published by the University of Georgia Press

Athens, Georgia 30602

www.ugapress.org

© 2011 by Iain Haley Pollock

All rights reserved

Designed by Walton Harris

Set in 10/15 Garamond Premier Pro

Printed digitally in the United States of America

Library of Congress Cataloging-in-Publication Data

Pollock, Iain Haley.

Spit back a boy : poems / by Iain Haley Pollock.

x, 78 p. ; 22 cm.

ISBN-13: 978-0-8203-3908-5 (pbk. : alk. paper)

ISBN-10: 0-8203-3908-3 (pbk. : alk. paper)

I. Title.

PS3616.O5696S65 2011

811'.6 — dc22   2010049358

British Library Cataloging-in-Publication Data available

For Naomi . . .

. . . and with thanks to Mom, Dad, and Caitlin

Contents

SPIT BACK A BOY

Rattla cain't hold me

Day levels to dusk, and they remind us
of rolled-down windows, night breezing through,
of driving nowhere, mileposts like drifting sparks

along the darkened shoulder, of R&B hooks
they emptied from their lungs like the rotting sweet
of old mess from a vase. We will lose them.

And all our sadness will be old Arkansas,
rural and misspoken, its roads smudged
by the fog's blue prints, its pine board shacks

daubed with mud to keep out mosquitoes
and the cold. The kitchens and porches
where we aren't will cease to exist. We'll miss

rain in autumn dousing the fire of the leaves,
wind writhing like a water moccasin.
Like convicts we'll sing, *Rattla cain't hold me*

Rattla cain't hold me, while outside the fence,
poplars, stripped by gypsy moths, stand bare.

Port of Origin: Lancaster

A group of Igbo linked arms
    and walked off Jamaica
into the Caribbean, cannibal sea.
    Behind them, the wind's *susu*
in arrows of bourbon cane,
    overpowering nectar
of boiling houses, tang of iron
    in door hinges and horse bits,
in manacles and flintlocks.
    When salt swallowed breath,
Igbo souls leapt from the water
    as great sea eagles. Talons gripped
black bodies as a she-bear lifts
    her cub by the scruff. Wings
throbbed air until all passed back
    to Igboland. I knew this,
knew before I heard
    the stories, read the books,
knew from the whispering
    of my black mother's blood
into my marrow. Knew also
    the mocking tap of rain
on the hull christened
    in my white father's city.
Knew how the ship lolled
    and pitched. How timbers
creaked. Creaked and creaked.
    All night, creaked. All day
that was night, creaked.
    Over dull slap of waves
on brine-soaked wood, creaked.

Over groans from hunger and
foul air and flux and lost sisters,
    creaked. Creaked and creaked
in the hollow chamber of a boy's ear —
    creaked, timbers creaked.

The Recessive Gene

Some neighborhood kids wondered
why I didn't look more like Mom,
and my friend Amilca told them:
We all black on the inside.

Dad had a pocketknife
I'd seen him use to quarter
apples and dig out their seeds.
That afternoon, I stole it.

Alone, behind the locked door,
I tried to scrape, as if fish scales,
the rosy skin from my forearms.

Hart Crane as Jim Crow

I was wrong. You weren't a madman,
just a minstrel without burnt cork
or the courage to steal chickens.

At the East River, eyeing the barely
men who reminded you of Ohio
before the fall, you finally understood

the acetylene burn of progress,
the elemental rupture of the age,
inferno lit on fuse of pure air.

But you were too far gone then
to raise an alarm against it — loathing
had spread into lymph and bone.

And so you called to the man-made myth
of the sky and praised the Juggernaut
that crushed you, added a plaque

to the cairn of steel and empire
that buried you day by day. Hart,
your bridge was framed in tar

and sugar. Its hum of traffic,
the pulse of cane knife
through stalk. And the rum

that helped you through the hurricane
was, like Communion wine, spiked
with blood. But you knew this, didn't you,

who died a slave's death over the side
of a ship? Rest, Hart, raging mask,
rest with the Atlantic and her dead.

At River Rock Farm

He was a man: hauled feed buckets,
built sheds to shelter his herd from heavy snow,
wrangled quarter-ton calves by their necks.
With a box of Jon's ashes, his kid brother

stood by a cow path that led to a wide bend
in a brook, and when I stepped up
to take my share, I thought the ash
would feel like fine beach sand. It didn't —

thick with tooth or shank, like so much
gravel washed onto the bank. I was sick
to know again some piece of my friend
and let loose the ash in a motion too familiar,

salting a stew, then watched the cinders
float past a stand of reeds, straw colored,
seed heads broken in descending height,
pipes in a cathedral organ. Going to rinse

my hand in the water, I stopped.
Cold, late fall wind rippled the surface.
A Hereford, penned in a far pasture,
lowed out, and I rubbed the trace of dust

into my palm, though I knew better
than to think it could permeate. Or stay.

Chorus of X, the Rescuers' Mark

X say search party, say month,

say day, X say live wire,

say gas leak, say floodwater,

say dead dog, dead cat,

X say no dead bodies,

say one dead body, say two,

say three dead bodies, say four,

X say kitchen, say bedroom, say attic,

say the family Bible floated next to me

five days before the waters carried it off,

X say that dog was a loud-ass, mean-ass bitch anyway,

say rain & wind on the roof was like every song

I ever heard, the slow & angry, the Sunday ones

& off-tune, pretty ones & ones that whined

like a porch door hanging on busted hinges, played

all together on harp, on fiddle, tuba, trumpet,

on banjo, on every instrument man saw fit to make,

X say Lord you been flooding us too much,

say most of the family moved north & west, got tired

of humidity & high water, called when they could,

say if you loot this you only stealin from Nature

& that bitch always take back what hers,

X say it got easier to die in water than live on land,

say you missed me buried under plaster & paint shreds

& wall stud & door & shingle & pictures of my grandbabies,

say we here & you never be rid of us,

say my worst sins were pride & white lies I recited

every morning like momma's daily prayers,

X say lungs full of flood in the end

took me higher than liquor ever did,

say blackwater love me more than my daddy ever did,

say pestilence, say quarantine, say lamb's blood,

say slave ship, say witch trials, say the Washita River

ran cold and the Cheyenne were still sleeping,

say the monk doused himself in gasoline,

say God, say man, say

                    not all of us are saved.

upon irremediable shores, those who never had time

We see the hunt of a cardinal, male,
more flamboyant for digging in the snow
after seeds set loose in the blizzard.

In the powder's mute and stop-motion, nothing
but the beating of the clock, replica of Victoria Station,
1905. Here's the real memory: on Olvera Street

I bought a marionette of Pancho Villa
riddled with nine bullets. And the false:
during my ninth birthday party, I swung

at a piñata mâchèd into Christ's burning heart
crowned with a thicket of blackberry thorns.
If we broke open this heart with a broomstick,

what sweetness would fall into the dust?
Does it matter that my family has no history

of senility or dementia? The women,
those with no fondness for tobacco,
live forever. The men die of mustard gas,
the Old Crow brand of bourbon, arrest —

cardiac or criminal. Oh, but my mother jigged
with Jim Crow once: first little black girl

to sit downstairs, not in *nigger heaven*, and butter
her face with popcorn at *That Darn Cat!*

the Lee Theater, Hampton, Virginia.
Preacher from a church where
she worshipped not deemed her

historical. And me, how will the holy
spirits diagnose me? And the real:
Batter my Wounded Knee. And the false:
Bury my heart at three person'd God.

The Frog

The house, new to us, white siding dinged with dirt,
black shutters, gaps between tar-paper shingles.

The split-rail fence in back greened with weather.
Splotches of rust around its bolts, the swing set sagged.

My parents sided with my sister. Mad, I huffed
into the yard. A two-trunked white cedar. Work shed

with cracked window. Tar-paper shingles. A frog —
tiny, green, translucent, almost camouflaged in chickweed

and crabgrass — hid near a fence post. My first stamp
missed. Splotches of rust around its bolts, the swing set

sagged. The frog's neck bloated twice with breath. Mad,
I drove the blunt force of my body. Black shutters.

Cracked window. Two-trunked cedar. My second stamp
snapped against the ground. Almost camouflaged,

chickweed, crabgrass. The frog — tiny. Splotches
of rust around its bolts, the swing set sagged.

Child of the Sun

Great Great Aunt Aida
trained her lapdog
to attack dark-skinned men.
A shake of her *high-yaller* head
and a suck on her ivory teeth,
and the Scottish terrier slipped
through the fence pickets
to nip at a *tar baby's* ankles.

Somewhere in her heaven,
Aunt Aida fusses today:
the lightest Haley yet,
naked to the waist
in a plastic lawn chair,
I'm a line cook browning
limbs in a skillet's thick oil,
a tanner of calf hide
curing skin in the sun.

Aida dreamed the family
would fade into a whiteness
of table manners and book learning,
and with me she came close.
But Mom must have eaten
a pig's foot when she was pregnant,
or dialed up the volume on those
Aretha records. Or I took it too hard,
that time in the grocery store

when a woman confused Mom
for my nanny — I bronze in the yard
all afternoon, hoping to blind
my eyes with scales and molt
like a sidewinder, to leave behind
a trail of skin, brittle, flaking, and white,
cracking and split in the sun.

Second Line

I put on a Mingus record, *Blues*
and Roots, after my grandfather died
and rummaged through an old wine box

that held my family photos. In my favorite,
Granddad was on all fours, playing the pony.
I'd fallen off his back, into the tall grass

of a Maryland yard, and sat cross-legged
near him. My memories of this, jazz
swept into them — I began to think

what I like about the best of Mingus:
how the players, confined by music, keep
probing, trying to puncture form and song,

the way a wire hanger in a garbage bag
stretches and tears at black plastic. The men
run their fingers and tongues along the bars

that separate sanity and chaos, meaning
and unmeaning. On that album Jackie McLean
led the charge. He was mostly ink in liner notes to me,

the man jazz cats called Jackie Mac. I only knew
that he shared my grandfather's name, that his sax —
I loved it, threatening to surge beyond the orbit

of Mingus's bass — that his playing narrated
my sadness. But Jackie's alto wasn't all mourning:
deep in his tone, a joyful second line — in the photo

Granddad's face was broad and fixed with laughter.

Longing as Hoppin John

From ecstatic blue flameburst of coiled burners,
the rising funk of black-eyed peas & collards.
Remember when we staked ourselves here
in this small, open kitchen, sated with light?
Not to hem appetites grown ragged
but to be transfigured like spice —
ground into cumin or cayenne,
mixed with slides of onion
& smoke of ham hocks
stirred in, steeped, stewed,
simmered to sauce,
spilled over rice,
folded by spoon,
again & again,
into grains of
soon &
yes.

Oya in Old City

i ain't Nigga Mary,
shrieks the red-bone woman
wearing two coats and sitting on a bench
along the Parkway when I mumble,
how are you? at her. And on the trip back
from Reading Market, she's leaning
against the fence to a baseball diamond
at Von Colln and raving: *dont let em fool you*
we aint win the Civil War   we still fightin
that shit. Watching her, I slip again
into the summer after second grade
when my mother drove me,
her half-breed son, into Philadelphia
to see the Liberty Bell and the black faces
she worried were too few in our dairy town,
where most color was her kin.
Draggling over cobblestones shadowed
by the spires of Independence Hall,
a rheumy-eyed bag lady — midnight black,
narrow shoulders widening to a paunch —
towed a trash-packed handcart
that clattered with each lopsided roll.
I stared at her, her three-whiskered mole,
until she seemed one of the goddesses,
bare breasted and round bellied,
squatting along my mother's bureau.
I think now I enjoyed her strangeness,
her possible divinity, but was terrified too
that she had the means, under her red shawl
or in the billow of plastic bags jouncing
in her cart, to destroy a boy like me.

The woman caught me gawking. She curled
her face to ugly, jabbed out her tongue,
and taunted me in a drawl thick with South:
take a motherfuckin picture   aint you never
seen a nigga. I flung my almost-white self
into my mother's embrace — that brown
embrace I hoped would swallow me whole
and spit back a boy four shades darker —
while the woman chuntered away, her cart
rattling over cobbles worn by centuries of traffic.

Hard Bop for Poor Boy

Dream Songhai   Dream Shango of thunder

Dream cicatrix   Dream Costo do Ouro   Dream

termite mounds   white ants   yourself devoured

Dream Virginia & piney woods   tobacco hung

from rafters   Dream carnage of angels   Dream polestar

Dream drapetomania   Dream cypress swamp

moon in water like a milk drop on mother's breast

Dream barred owl & copperhead   cur & bloodhound

Babe   I cain't stay here long/

Dream muddy waters of Jordan   Dream homestead

chickens roosting in the sweet gum   Dream clapboard

& mule skinning   cigar box   gutbucket   Dream

bottomlands flooding   Dream High John de Conqueror

Dream hex   Dream devils & *haints*   nickel buried buffalo up

Dream night riders   Dream torch & shroud-laid rope

Babe   I cain't stay here long/

Dream Illinois Central   Union Station   Dream brick

& rust   redlined   Darktown   sourness of rotting   Dream

meatpacking & steel furnace   flat-iron & gas stove   *last hired,*

first fired   Dream dice & that same pot liquor   that same sermon

& shout   Dream Red Summer   Dream that same truncheon

Dream *badge up North hide a white man how a white hood do*

down South   same pistol-whip & dog snarl   *Don't look em*

in the eye — they quick to shoot   Dream revolver   that same   revolver

revolver   that same   revolver   that same   Dream

    Babe   I cain't stay here long/

    I'ma Poor boy   long way from home/

    Poor boy and a long way from home/

Killadelphia

pop ^{pa} pop-pop

                           pop,

and before sirens echo

      echo

               echo
up streets laid out
      like wire mesh in a pen

      where pit bull
      bitches — three,
      chained, starved —
      lurch scarred
      throats into yowls,

sneaker soles slap-clap
on asphalt
until their stride
sinks

      into rumble-grumble
      of daybreak
      trolleys trundling
      down steel tracks,

newsprint smack-
thwacking, pitched
onto gum-mottled
pavement at corner markets

security gates
flung up in a rickety-
racket at Mt. Zion's
storefront worship,

skittery-skitter
of boys kicking
a doll's head
to the bus stop,

molded lids
ticking open
and shut
over glazed
unreal eyes,

raccoon's crash-
dash as it drags
a near-dead pigeon
from a rust-pitted
trash can,

fluttery-stutter
of the bird's
one good wing
flapping to lift
its carcass into
                    still-darksome dawn

The Lieutenant, Returned

At night
he'd rather piss

in the coin jar
than scuffle

down the hall
to the toilet

without his flak
jacket & rifle.

Snow in Wartime

It's warm for Syracuse in deep December —
but still cold enough for snow, snow made
light and fat by a sweep over Lake Ontario,
the flakes like down from a split pillow.
We're walking on the western shore of Onondaga,
hand in hand, the few towers on the skyline
visible through spare trees. The path runs
between dense beds of common reeds —
invading marshy ground around the lake —
and tumbledown docks of ruined resort hotels.

Before the snow I was thinking: *What a rabbit
punch, this month*. Painkillers and chemotherapy
thinning your uncle's voice. Granddad gone
a second winter, again no Lancashire *hullo*.
Our friend's pickup rolled off an icy road —
his neck snapped. The list of more boys,
from whistle-stop towns in Texas, Pennsylvania,
Ohio, dead. Car bombs in Baghdad
and Kufa ending six-dozen unnamed lives.

But while the lake effect falls, I stop worrying
about illness and accidents and war and stand
with you to watch the slow drift. Years from now,
we'll forget that I hardly talked with you,
that Mack trucks growled nearby, that death
choked at our thoughts. I'll remind you then —
faced with dope-addicted daughter
or father's congestive collapse — that once
there was a lake where we walked together,
fingers intertwined, the sky hushed to snow.

On the Porch, Almost Men

Night couldn't break the day's humidity.
We sat on the warped top step of the porch,

gas station cigars burning in our fingers,
girls kindling in our minds. *It must've*

slipped off once, he confessed, *the rubber.*
We drew smoke into our mouths

while mosquitoes and moths spiraled
between us. An Olds — a Cutlass — crawled by,

then the road returned to weak moonlight.
She went . . . He stopped, a bead of sweat

rolled down his temple and along his jaw. *I think
it's gone.* On cigars' stub ends, we flared

orange signals into the dark. Across the street
whitewashed apartments, lamps out for the night,

looked blankly back at us. He let a waft
of smoke float from his mouth and turned

his head toward the lilac bush — the blooms,
flaked brown, clung to their stems. *She won't*

let me touch her now . . . In the shadow
and porch light, his profile jutted like the beams

of a house, half-burnt and abandoned.

Medusa of Libya

he used my ugliness against me. no,
my fear of ugliness hiding in the crags

and outcroppings of this volcanic stone.
lord, my charms had tamed horses

and the sea. i'd had a queen's power
to transmute men. but he held sway

over me with the warp of polished bronze.
i saw there what i'd suspected: my nose,

a snout. my smile, twin rows of fangs.
my wisdom grown to a beard. my plaits,

a tangled nest of vipers. as a girl my pupils
were ringed with brown ripe as dates —

his mirror reminded them of betrayal,
betrayal like a lover's, sudden, stony.

my three gray sisters share one good eye:
why did the gods bless them with blindness,

me with a doubtful gaze? o, to have never seen,
in his bronze, my face disgusting as maggots

worming in goat's meat. or worse, his eyes —
to have never seen them glassy with rage and dread,

their cruel and terrified beauty the last i'd know.

Flight

The Aaron boys
have brilliant African names:
Shango, Bu, Amilca, Oginga.
Above our apartment block,

from an embankment crowned
with pueblo-style town houses
plastered in faux adobe,
Bu and Shango fire rocks

at the younger of us. Crouching
in the sparse cover of scrub
and imported pines, Mil, Ging, and I
rise and return salvos of gravel

and dirt clods — the goal isn't to hit
the target, just a near miss to make
eyes bulge like grapes pushed
from their skin or force a shriek

we'd find girlish and laugh at later.
Townhouse roofs lining the ridge form
an audience of furrowed, terra-cotta brows
while we scrabble up and down the slope,

trip in the skein of crawling brush,
drop quickly to our bellies
when bulleting rocks come close.
Errant throws from the battle fly over

low adobe walls behind the townhouses
and skid across their concrete patios.
We dodge and laugh and yell
and don't notice a white woman

wrench open her sliding glass door
and rampage into her enclosed yard:
If you throw one more rock, I'll call the police
on you little fuckers.
                    Five hundred years kick in:

we scatter

            like Angola boys

                        from the first Portuguese —

Confirmation

Mikey Clark liked to do otherwise:
he called teachers by their first names,
scrounged smoldering butts off the ground

and smoked them to yellowed filters,
broke the lock to the fallout shelter in the old gym
and took his girl of the month there after school,

goaded the Perkins brothers into confession
and lifted a jug of Communion wine from St. John's
while Father Rubinsky heard their phony sins,

pulled a cap gun on Artie at Artie's Gas,
making off with pocketfuls of Tootsie Rolls
and a weekend's supply of chips and soda.

During a February thaw sophomore year,
Mikey, out of his skull on ecstasy, slipped
climbing to a Bluff party, landed on his back

in the creek bottom. At the funeral Kevin
and Charlie Perkins wore ties, castoffs
from their father with pulls in the silk.

Behind us, Nina Conti's grandmother recited,
like a devotional, that evil comes in threes,
but before we graduated, four other boys

would die — an accident out on Route 5,
two suicides with closets and bedsheets,
one with Bud Light cans and a father's .38.

After the Mass Father Rubinsky
approached my friends and me to share
comforting words about God's will and flocks

and Mikey, then ruffled our hair, thanked us
for wearing church clothes and marveled,
since confirmation, at how much we'd grown.

King Biscuit Time

featuring Sonny Boy Williamson
a.k.a. Rice Miller, a.k.a. Alec Miller

As many names as towns between Glendora
and Helena. As bits of cotton floating
in a freshly picked field. But he wanted
to be the best, so he stole from the best —

Sonny Boy. *Your funeral and my trial*:
he emptied the name and filled it
with ache and alcohol, with lonesome cabins

and left-behind women. Hustling flour on the radio
with a counterfeit name beat breaking his back
in a field he didn't own. Every afternoon,

King Biscuit Time, he brought the juke's unbridled
dance of air and reed and tongue to day,
blowing his harp hard enough to reach
from Memphis to the Mississippi Sound,

to cut through static hissing like pig fat
in cast iron. The way he bent notes,
the Blues harp became a plowshare —

he burrowed it below the ear where neck
meets jaw 'til laughing and crying sounded
struck from the same steel, 'til all 'croppers

who heard could feel the joy of quitting time
throbbing along the seams of their skulls,
'til they knew why the Lord made the forgiveness
of night: for soaking sore joints in corn liquor,

for blotting out Delta Sun, hot
as a branding iron, for pistol-whipping
the Blues back down into the dust and mud

that raised them up, for hoping to wake reborn
with a name better than *mule* and a freedom
more lasting than crop cycles or a man's breath

wailing through metal chambers of a harp.

Appalachia

Sun slipping behind the Appalachians
lit mountaintops, their oaks & hickories,

like signal fires. You'd kicked off your sandals,
& on the slope the old hatchback chortled hard

under your bare foot. With each press of gas,
your sundress, a pattern of crescents in white

& brown & peach shaded pale, rode higher
up your tensed thigh. I'd fallen long before,

but your dress for a day's drive & picturing
how that last sunlight filtered through the canopy

& flecked onto laurel & rosebay in the understory —
that sure didn't make my heart any colder.

My Stove's in Good Condition

Because she thought I wanted it,

> for dinner Naomi wants catfish,
> > catfish on the range spitting oil, its smoke
> > > spicing the house with pepper, black & cayenne.

From speakers in the living room, ragtime piano,

> a winking old blues by Lil Johnson,
> > Lil Johnson singing about her stove but fooling
> > > with more than pots & pans: *When my wood gets too hot . . .*

I check the crisp on the fish & flip, then shuffle in my slippers

> to the front windows, looking for Naomi to pull up at the house,
> > brick house down the street from the Poplar Bridge,
> > > built in '22 & crumbling over the freight rail line.

No sign of her little blue car,

> just the 32 bus ferrying riders from North Philly,
> > North Philly to graveyard shifts downtown,
> > > guards & clerks & cleaners in the lit cabin

like relatives waiting in a hospice room:

> a man presses his forehead against a window,
> > window pushing up the brim of his cap: a gray woman
> > > slouches down & pillows her head on plastic bags stuffed

with plastic bags & piled on the next seat. Watching for Naomi,

I'd lost the fish & music, then again the crackling,
　　crackling of cornmeal & pepper, of Lil Johnson
　　　　& her lusty blues: *Nothin to be waitin on, let's get drunk*

and truck. A month since we lay curled & sweaty in bed:

　　on the way back to the kitchen, I turn down the music,
　　　　music that growled like hunger, growled like the dull ache
　　　　　　of hunger filling the body, pushing out till the mind

pricks with hunger, is consumed with hunger —

so much hunger in these blues:
　　　　　　　　blues so much hunger:
　　　hunger so much blues:
　　　　　　　　　　　　　so much blues:
　　　　hunger:
　　　　　　　　　　　　hunger:
so much:
　　　　　　　　blues:
　　　hunger so much:
　　　　　　　　blues:
　　　so much:
　　　　　　　　blues:
　　hunger:
　　　　　　blues

Black Irish

Sixteen hours hence, on the water closet floor at the inn, I'll vomit in the
    shape of the Congo (country, the big one, not river),
and Naomi, who at first accuses me of indulging in an excess of Jameson and
    Guinness, will realize I'm sick
and take pity on me by wiping the floor with the pajama bottoms I'm
    inexplicably no longer wearing and am forced to abandon in Ireland.
All I have is stomach flu, but the name we've used for the bouts of sickness
    laying low wedding guests and the bride
is winter vomiting, a more serious illness, and when I explain to the
    attendant on the flight stateside that I have *a touch of winter vomiting*,
her arms flap with fear — I'll need to be quarantined for forty days on this
    godforsaken island (*godforsaken* sprang to mind
as I choked yellow-green gall into a black garbage bag for the sixth time
    during the hour ride to Shannon's airport).
But at present Naomi and I wander on the outskirts of a fishing village,
    along a narrow, hedge-lined road running parallel to a stream.
The water flows over a bed of mossy rocks into the Atlantic, an Atlantic
    related to the ocean *down the shore* back home
but like its anguished older brother, brooding over the coast, casting a layer
    of steel wool over the stone houses and shops.
Across the road a donkey grazes on tufts of grass in a field, and because I
    associate Ireland with cops and books
(beer would be stereotypical, and the time's before noon), and because as a
    black boy I learned a healthy fear and disdain of all police —
though I've had nothing but helpful run-ins with the law (likely because I'm
    often confused for white),
as when earlier this week in the rain, golf umbrella impairing my sight, a
    black boy pulled a gun (chrome appearing in the streetlight
like a shark from the depths of an aquarium tank) and took my wallet, and a
    black (not black Irish, but black black — in Philadelphia

we have a black mayor and many a black) cop came to the house and calmed
   me down and made me feel safe —

I ask my wife if she can guess the donkey's name, and when she can't, I
   punch-line: (*Donkey*)*xote*, and Naomi rolls her eyes, and I find myself
   cracking myself up.

Shot & Killed

A detective banged on my door
at two in the morning
and asked if I'd heard gunfire:

a teenage boy in the neighborhood
had been shot and killed.
He pointed up the street,

and right away I knew
which house. Last month,
I'd spent a half hour
with my field guide

figuring out its backyard tree
was a Kentucky coffee,
short empty pods hanging
from the stark branches like bats.

I'd also seen the boy around,
waiting on the corner
for the school bus, his knit cap
laced with melting snow.

But I hadn't heard any shots.
And I never learned the boy's name.

BLUE NOTE 53428

They'd picked a green. They'd cleared
a room. His guitars, beads and spools of wire
for her jewelry trucked to the basement.
The night they'd guessed it happened,
"Blue Train" was on 'RTI. The song
was Boston, where he'd bought the album,

played it again and again, their setting-out days,
Kenmore Square, that eat-in kitchen, furnished
with finds from Goodwill, chairs upholstered
with orange vinyl, Formica table she'd sat on once,
back from the bar, when they'd kissed until their lips

bruised, her heels locked behind his knees, their bodies
like roots of riverside sycamores left exposed by high water.
A helicopter chops low over their row of houses,
and windows rattle in their casements. They'd picked

a green. They'd cleared a room. Three mornings ago,
she'd cramped and bled. Cramped and bled
on sheets blue as the bright sky that's making her
sick now. Same sick as when the dogwood dropped

its white petals, leaving only leaves. They'd cleared
a room. They'd picked a green — good choice,
they'd heard, good choice for boy or girl . . .

Burn Pile

There was a road, hard packed — then came
the negation of road.
                              Surrounding the crater,
roots of palm trees and streetlamps.
                                              Smoke
and exposed rebars grimaced out of concrete.

Cars, burnt chassis or flipped on their roofs,
like a row of upturned beetles in the wake
of some torturous boy.
                              The façades of restaurants
and auto shops heaped, damming water that erupted
from pipes and mains.
                              The cloth of tattered stalls
fluttering as vans and trucks careened on their way
to dig screams from the rubble.
                                      A hand — charred, red,
without arm in the wreckage.
                                      These images, a year
or more ago, broadcast from somewhere beyond
the silhouette of treetops, the expressway's dull rush.

Here, seedpods helicopter off the sugar maple
and land in mown grass.
                              The family next door
has lost its rottweiler again, and the father
walks up the hill calling: *Diesel   Come on Diesel
here girl   Diesel.*
                      At the end of autumn,
these neighbors will build their burn pile too high.

Flames will singe the underside of branches
and threaten to top the high pickets separating
our yards.
            But for today, under shade trees, lounging
on aluminum lawn chairs, forcing Florida limes
down the necks of our beer bottles, we drink outdoors

until dusk, when mosquitoes, droning like far-off propellers,
chase us behind the wire screen to the closed-in porch.

and your young men shall see visions . . .

Growing up, the girls, black and white,
only played with rosy-skinned dolls,
blondes at that, never brunettes. Walking

to McGolrick Park, I see a black doll,
a clump of her braids caught in the razor wire
of a shuttered tile store, kitchen and bath,

its grimy, galvanized security door locked
this Sunday morning. On a park bench,
Naomi and I sit with her brother and eat

an apple pie we've carried from the other side
of the BQE, under eighteen-wheelers barraging
down the viaduct. Crust and glazed filling

are surprisingly warm, given our trek,
like the day, late November, is warm,
surprisingly. Six boys play tackle

with a football that's too fat for their hands,
and the team with the biggest boy,
cornrows out, hair hanging to his shoulders,

seems to score a touchdown every time.
A pigeon flock wheels overhead, and talking
not to each other, but to their Pomeranian,

either a scold or a coo, a scruffy young couple
brunches on a ragged quilt under nearly unclad
plane trees while old Poles straggle home

from church, ten feet behind them a trail
of daughters, dressed in black and smoking,
husbandless and cloudy as the day should be.

The boys have shifted to a leaf pile
across the park. Yawps and shrieks
of their wrestling rise through scattered

seed clusters still swaying on mottled limbs
and meet the pigeons as they dip and veer.
When the big boy yells, *Let's bury us*

an come up in ten minutes, they agree,
the smaller boys, flopping into the mound,
rustling down toward the softening ground,

the mud there, my own autumns tell me,
bearing the shape, the lobes and teeth,
the veins of broad and fallen leaves.

Queen of the Lower Ninth

Kassiopeia, your beauty
warmed the air, jasmine,
the language of lost temples.

When the sea grew jealous,
you chided him:
Sea, you is ugly.

Sea, you is a whore choked with the devil's short hairs.
And the sea flew at you,
masculine, suffocating.

Your voice rasped like wilderness.
Like the whine of trapped furs.
Necromantic.

The sea snaked up your ankles,
stirruped them with fingers evil as tar,
pried apart the roundness of your thighs.

The levy broke into a current of scales.
Can't sorrow and pity me out of my stead.
But the winged man in guise

of healer stole your daughter,
stole her in the name of the sea,
then receded, turning magnolias

to stone, flowering infection.
And your throat forgot laughter,
spluttered like a cracked engine.

Your hair snarled and tangled
in stretching crow's feet. Your teeth
ground themselves to lime.

After centuries of glimmer, your eyes
stormed: *Give me back my bones, ugly,*
you howled into the public phone.

Kassiopeia,
proud Ethiop queen:
and the wind still stings with salt.

Northbound

Down the rail line parallel to this footpath, a commuter train
shuttles north past the bulrushes of the land-filled estuary.
Broad river this side of the tracks, bluffs on the other warp
the engine's horn and rush into a sound like the squawk

of a boy's broken fire truck. Naomi loves how breeze
from the Hudson brushes through sorrel and rockrose gripping
the bank, but today she walks ahead on the trail, her anger with me
lengthening her stride toward the lot and our car. Beyond her,

two men — facing the water, hands dovetailed between them —
break off a sly kiss. Spinning around, they jaunt past us
and flirt down the path to the shoreline where our spat
began. I should remember most days we are like them, playful

and loving in public. The train isn't far off now — it roars
and rifles by, headed upriver, Peekskill, Garrison, Cold Spring . . .

Camphor

White butterflies, fluttering over poppies,
opened and closed their wings
like unsure hands in prayer. Margaret's head
propped on his shoulder, Jack watched
a stray white flit to a row of cabbage.
When a car in a nearby drive kicked up
a rattle of stones, he laid her head
onto the pillow. Red-blonde strands
seeped across the blue-checked case.

Their firstborn had died in infancy,
Jack's father from breaths of mustard gas
drawn in the Great War. This time,
no one lingered in the hallway; no one
waited downstairs in the parlor: university,
ocean, grave kept their children away,
his brother knelt over sheep
for summer shearing, she the last Fisher
and he hadn't rung the neighbors.

No hand rested on Jack's shoulder
while he felt Margaret's cancered lungs
rasp out their air onto the buckled column
of his neck. Then, in the road,
a pack of boys called wildly
into the twilight while around him
Jack smelled camphor, guarding
their wool and silk against moths,

and he arrived at the farmhouse step —
branches of an old ash swaying across
shadows thrown by dim window lights —
to wait for a hired girl who would come out
the heavy door to walk the stone-walled lanes.

The Diaspora Remembers Guantánamo

I know you longed for a woman's fingers
to pull the knots from your hair. I know

the sea smelled of iron and smoke. I know,
wanting to dream pomegranates, you saw

only strange fruit. I know your God
was silent in this place. You stripped the beds

until your lungs burned. Your heart fevered
to be free of the body's closet. Your sight

turned purple as the desert rose. I know.
In the dark you saw a maroon's head,

severed, then caged. As your neck
cinched to windpipe, I know your shadow

scored into the concrete. On this coast
where, gaunt and moaning, I clattered in cuffs,

I know — and my veins open like a grass basket
to store your name with the grain of my memory.

Eastern State Penitentiary

A robin settles
outside the sentry box
on a gray rail streaked
with fingers of rust.
On weather-cragged stones,
a berry — red gone brown,
roundness shrunken
and dimpled by winter —
dangles from a creeping vine.

Useless as an empty
birthing chair,
this Quaker experiment
to restore inmates' *virtue
and happiness*, to *unbosom
their souls with freedom,*
holds a museum now,
asters and butterfly bush
in flowerbeds along its walls,

and when a docent leads me
into a moldering cellblock,
raw, perennial damp —
still trapped in the mortar —
tightens my lungs.
This must have been true
for them too: the horse thieves
and pickpockets sat alone
in these rooms, heads down,
slumped against gneiss and schist
or, occupied with forced labor,

cobbling shoes, weaving clothes
they'd never wear. Solitary,

they repented through industry
and prayer, submitted to God
in silence broken by the rants
and consumptive hacks
of fellow penitents echoing off
the vaulted ceilings. Fitted
with black hoods to leave
their cells, they saw only
His ever-watchful eye,
manifest as a band of sun
shining through a skylight,

His eye, a mute beauty
amid howls and hums
while men worked
or thought themselves mad,
His eye, more humane
than an ear slashed off,
than red ribbons of skin
flayed from the spine.

Looking Glass is dead.

In Idaho, the Nez Perce Forest,
while the fire's shadows played in overhanging
ponderosas, sudden flickers causing me
to flinch and turn toward the dark

behind my shoulders, I sat on a rotting log
and picked loose strands from the bristles
of my sister's comb. Though my father
cautioned me not to, I balled a handful
of her hair and threw the clutch

                                   into the flames.
At school that spring, a Holocaust survivor
told us human hair — that not shaved and packed
into pillowcases — human hair burning was the worst
smell she remembered. I hadn't believed her.
The smell couldn't have been much worse
than my mother's hair on the hot comb,

a little foul but tinged with jojoba
and shea butter. Not worse than garbage
souring in early August or the deer carcass
we'd hiked past.
                    I discovered, around that fire,
how wrong I was. But there were harder ways
to learn this: smoke incensed with my sister's hair
turned acrid as Auschwitz while it curled from the logs
and hung in the red pines of the Nez Perce.

The school-march, each day's festival

The rain has let up,
the school and grounds a shade darker
for the soaking. To leaves and bark on a holly

outside my classroom window, to the red roof,
to the red path and tulip trees lining it,
to a cherry sprouting ruffled pink across the road —

a heavy, dank beauty, a beauty I could not grasp
when I was like the boys screaming on the playing fields.
The right fielder spills into wet grass

while he backpedals to shag a lazy fly ball.
And the music teacher, her father dying
at Mercy-Fitz, walks down the path to her car.

Going to lunch, I'd held the door and envied
her raincoat while my sopping shirt clung
to my chest. I recognize her now by that coat,

her face covered by the dome of her umbrella,
slick and blue-black, saving her from the false rain
still dripping off the trees. When she rounds

the corner, wind kicks up, pulling blossoms
and leaf buds off branches, and the storm
starts in again. Boys scamper from the fields

and, not checking the road for cars as their cleats
clack a stampede on the dampened asphalt,
race under the eaves to the gym where they stand

shoulder to shoulder, each wriggling in his place
as if an innocent man leaned on a wall
and, with his own sweat-dark bandana, made blind.

Whale Song

Naomi hunches over the sink, in profile to me.
At the kitchen table, I pretend to solve a crossword

but watch her and how silly she looks
with a cloud of soap hanging in the bangs

over her forehead. Our refrigerator shakes
into the deep, haunting hum Naomi thinks beautiful,

and she cranes toward me, saying, *Oh, that's the whale song
again*, then lifts her eyes to the kitchen window,

filled with tilted light, to look at the patio garden,
the Virginia creeper gone orange. I smile

thinly and listen to the song, until a trolley car,
grinding around the dogleg in Girard Avenue,

drowns it out. The trolley thunders west, past the liquor store
and Happy Garden Chinese. When the rumble dies down,

the hum has stopped, and I tell Naomi, *That didn't sound
a thing like a whale*. She drops her sight from the window

and, reaching through the skim of suds in the steel basin,
takes the next dish. Head down, soap in her hair catches

the same light — early October — as spume on the lake
where I took a grey trout off the line, held it by the tail,

and stared, amazed with its gills' silent rippling,
with the struggle causing scales down its flanks to shimmer

like the stretch of pale sunset over choppy water, stared
until the fish slipped from my hand and, slapping off the dock,

disappeared under a moored boat, its dark hull.

Like a Blind Boy Jumping from Shed to Shed

Dad drove up on a couple arguing
in the street while Stevie Wonder warbled

"My Cherie Amour" on the radio. The man jabbed
his right finger into the woman's face, his own face

torqued into a scream. She tried to move past him,
but he blocked her with his broad, puffed chest,

and they left their footwork printed in the pollen
that maples, bursting with new leaves, had dusted

onto the road. Dad pulled his Chevette
between their bodies and told me, six,

to roll down my window. The woman leaned in,
her brown eyes like glass beads, and pleaded, *Dont let im*

bruise me   Not today. Stretching slantwise across the car,
Dad popped the lock. The woman clambered

into the backseat while the man, beating the roof
above our heads, screamed, *Dont you leave with her*

I'll break you both. But Dad eased out the clutch
and rolled the car toward D.C. rush hour.

The woman slurred sober directions, then didn't talk
till we pulled up to her building, just slumped

along the seat and bobbed her head to the beat,
the Howard station, WHUR, *Sounds Like Washington*, soul.

(So Tired of Standing Still We Got to) Move On

Years since
        I stumbled home
early morning,
        my body a cocktail
of cologne
        & dance-floor funk.
Standing now
        at the white door,
dirt streaking its panels
        like nickel-&-dime mascara,
standing now
        under a November sky
like a slabstone marker
        in a burial ground
I can't afford,
        standing now & looking
through a beech sapling's
        saw-toothed brown leaves
at the scrapes & peels
        in the silver paint
of the hail-pocked hood,
        I can't drive
to school, to teaching
        to another day
of spouting platitudes
        to inclement teenagers.
I feel already
        like the James Brown
of *Love Over-due*,
        late career, jaw distended

by liquor, coke
     & the forced indolence
of jail time,
     the paunch brimming
over his rhinestoned belt
     a burden
to once-upon snake hips,
     his relaxed hair
hardened
     to an unreal helmet
of dark quartz.

Turning the key,
     I click
the deadbolt into place
     & strut
with a half-limp
     to the rattle-boned car.
JB had to keep
     in the studio,
on the road:
     long after the magic
of invention,
     we keep doing
what we know
     or what we know
pays the bills.
     Yeah,
we keep doing
     what we do,
doing, doing
     what we do —
do, do, doing
     what we do.

Migratory Habits

> what Socrates,
> the hemlock hour nigh,
> told sorrowing
> Phaedo and the rest
> about the migratory
> habits of the soul.
>
> —ROBERT HAYDEN, "A Plague of Starlings"

I.

Like loops of black thread unspooled
on a sewing table, Route 6 winds uphill,

headed for the Bear Mountain Bridge.
The day swelters with heat that makes

cicadas whine, then ends in thunder's clap
and roll. On the radio a rambler picks

a haunting country blues from a dreadnought's
nickel strings, and Naomi, sitting in the driver's seat,

starts to cry: in England her uncle —
a girlhood confidant — is dying,

the cancer inoperable. Her grip tenses
on the steering wheel, and in my head

words flap and flutter as a sparrow
trapped and clamoring against a window.

Rubbing her arm, I hope the balm
of my touch will ease distance and sadness

better than my silence. Below, between sheer cliffs,
the Hudson snaking around Indian Point flows

toward the Narrows and beyond, the sea.

II.

In the yard, facing sundown,
Adirondack chairs we inherited

last summer from her parents
have faded to gray in the weather.

Naomi curls on a teakwood bench
in the front room and cries again,

the draws of breath between sobs sharp
as the night barks of a fox. Last week,

she watched her uncle — tubes
twining around him as woodbine

on a fence post — go slack.

Outside the window, a cardinal
with dark beak and brown young breast,

just a tinge of red in its wings,
lands to peck up the grass seed

that this morning we sowed
into the thin and yellowed lawn.

III.

Naomi and I lean against rough-hewn timbers
at Wolvercote Lock on the Oxford Canal,
north of the university. A side stream

bows around the stagnant lock
and gurgles back into the channel:
her uncle's air sounded like this water,

Naomi says, those final minutes, in the shallows
of his throat, before his breath dried out.
In the quiet after her witness, a moorhen,

bill a sudden red against its black feathers,
five chicks churning in its wake,
swims into the canal from behind a clump

of flagging purple irises. Downstream
the hen leads its young to the eastern shore,
then through sedge, bur reed, and hard rush,

to forage in the puddles of a fallow field,
and Naomi throws the whole of her body
into my body, and like taut rope hitched
around a wooden bollard, we hold.

Vertical Hold, 1967

A rising storm
pushed smoke,
from a burn pile
down the road,

across the yard and up
through the last, hardheaded
acorns of a red oak.
The boy shuffled his feet

where he thought
the foul line should be
and stared at a hoop

nailed to a chipped square
of plywood hung
from a telephone pole,
leaning and disused.
He tried to ignore

cars whipping
down Route 8, the sting
of leaf smoke, taunts
from his sister who spun

in a tire swing slung over
an oak branch, hesitant drops
as anvil clouds grew angrier.
He narrowed his sight
on the front of the rim,

on a spot where rusted metal
glared through a gash
in orange paint. When he
hurled up the ball,

the boy didn't follow
its arc through gray air
but, bouncing from foot
to foot, keeping his eyes
on the rickety hoop,

watched his shot
pinball on the rim
and waited to know
on what ground
his prayer would fall.

Affection

One Friday a month, my father pulled clippers —
Wahls — from a worn shoebox *to tighten*
my fade before the school dance. The cut
was accomplished with an economy of words
and movement:

                I'd sit quietly under his hand,
listening to the electric hum of the Wahls
while his precise strokes sent flurries of curls
to the bathroom floor and his light touch
on my chin rotated the angle of my head
left or right, up or down.

                    When he bent the tops
of my ears flat to shave behind them, I'd start
scraping fingernails against my thighs, the full power
of gravity keeping me in the red folding chair
until a gruff *How's it look?* and I'd shoot up
to preen for the mirror and inspect.

                        Once satisfied,
I'd stamped up to my room to dress for the night
while downstairs my father swept four week's worth
of hair from the floor tiles, the whisk of the corn broom
over linoleum sounding softly as the cradle song
that a child heavy with sleep only half hears.

Ne Me Quitte Pas

With a six-pack

I come to Rachel's studio,

where the stereo plays

        Nina Simone, *Live in Paris*,

indelibly sad, chains

     of an empty swing

in the wind

       creaking into a braid.

Marvin and Lamar sit for photos,

the dark crook

         of Marvin's arm

wrapped around Lamar's smooth,

sand-colored shoulder

          like a clasp

on a safety strap.

I've never been

       this close

to intimate men.

      But they're so boyish

and vulnerable with each other,

          I wonder

    how intimate they've been:

whispers

     in the halls say

        the Spanish teacher at school

has spent his life loving men

      but never

touching them.

     And watching Marvin

clutch Lamar,

     I think of all the *faggot*s

       in punchlines

that doubled me over,

    and the tirade of *faggot*s

     a kid unleashed

       in the locker room

that I pretended not to hear,

    the *at-least-I'm-not-a-faggot*

after Vaughn Curran

      called me *half-nigger*,

and all the *faggot*s

                    I thought were harmless

          because I mumbled them

                              only to my mind.

          From a stepladder

                    Rachel begins to pop

the flash,

              and a tear traces the ridge

                        of Marvin's cheekbone.

A stranded tear

          in bas-relief

against his ebony skin,

          a permissive tear

              teaching the tribe

to open.

Spring & the Catkins

Cloth pansies,
their yellow fading, planted
in the neighbor's flower box.

A Kenmore washer,
the model still in my parent's basement,
oxidating in a grassed-over lot.

Gray as newsprint in the rain,
a nest of paper wasps clinging
below the pussy willow's catkins.

I tried to accept these
as beautiful today and couldn't.
How did you choose

a life with me? How did you
forgive me for myself?

Beth David Cemetery, Long Island

I am the only man standing by the open grave
without a yarmulke, with dreadlocks spilling
onto the lapels of my suit jacket. Next to me
Naomi stares at her grandfather's coffin.

Under the distant roar of jets arcing
over the Sound, three workers speak
Caribbean Spanish, hushed and rapid, and smoke
while they wait to fill the grave, their backs to us
and the wind. On headstones nearby, mourners
have set rocks, a sign of the permanence
of their loss, and of the earth. And families
have hedged some plots with evergreens
to keep other funerals from trampling their dead.

Cousin Seymour, a slight, devout man, breaks
our silence — *We should be the ones to bury Jack,*
not them — and Naomi's father takes up a shovel
and steps toward his father's grave. I back away,
onto a gravel path, bristling to think that *them*
is the three grave diggers, that *them* is us, dark people.

But while the men and boys, passing the shovels
between them, cast dirt onto the coffin,
and the grave begins to fill with the smack
and roll of dirt clods on the casket lid,
while Will, a great-grandson, struggles
to balance a load of soil on a shovel blade,

I recognize that Seymour meant *them* who are not
us, our family, *them* not fused with us by life
and faith, who do not suffer now when we
have cause to suffer. And as our family leaves
for the reception and the days of sitting shiva,
I know that when I die, our children, our grandchildren,
they will grieve for me with shovels and their hands.

Notes on the Poems

"Rattla cain't hold me": Title and lines "Rattla cain't hold me / Rattla cain't hold me" are taken from a line in the work song "Judy," found on *Wake Up Dead Man* (recorded by Bruce Jackson, Rounder Records, 1994).

"upon irremediable shores, those who never had time": Title of the poem is taken from Édouard Glissant's epigraph to *Chronicle of the Seven Sorrows* (Omaha: University of Nebraska Press, 1999), Patrick Chamoiseau's first novel. Glissant's passage originally appears in his book *Caribbean Discourse*.

"Second Line": Charles Mingus's *Blues and Roots* first appeared in 1960 from Atlantic Records.

"Hard Bop for Poor Boy": The repeated lines after each stanza are from the blues song "Poor Boy," performed by various musicians, including Bukka White and R. L. Burnside. The lines here are adapted from Howlin' Wolf's version.

"King Biscuit Time": "Your funeral and my trial" is a line from Sonny Boy Williamson's "Your Funeral and My Trial," found on *The Essential Sonny Boy Williamson* (MCA/Chess, 1993).

"My Stove's in Good Condition": Title of the poem is the title of a Lil Johnson song that appears on the compilation *1936–1937 'Hottest Gal in Town'* (Story of the Blues, 1991). The line "when my wood gets too hot" is taken from this song. The line "nothing to be waitin on, lets get drunk and truck" is taken from her song "Let's Get Drunk and Truck," which appears on the same album. Authorship of this song is not attributed.

"BLUE NOTE 53428": Title of the poem is the Blue Note Records catalog number for John Coltrane's *The Ultimate Blue Train* (1997).

"and your young men shall see visions . . .": Title of the poem is taken from Joel 2:28, found in *The New Oxford Annotated Bible*, 3rd ed. (Oxford: Oxford University Press, 2001).

"Eastern State Penitentiary": Both quotes in the poem are found in Michael Meranze, *Laboratories of Virtue: Punishment, Revolution, and Authority in Philadelphia, 1760-1835* (Chapel Hill: University of North Carolina Press, 1996); "virtue and happiness" (2) originally appeared in the constitution of the Philadelphia Society for Alleviating the Miseries of Public Prisons; "unbosom their souls with freedom" (261) first appeared in the Commissioners to Superintend the Erection of the Eastern State Penitentiary, *Letter Report and Documents*.

"Looking Glass is dead.": Title is taken from a speech given by Hin-mah-too-yah-lat-kekt (Chief Joseph the Younger) of the Nez Perce after the Battle of Big Paw in 1877. The speech expresses the leader's desire to surrender to General Oliver O. Howard of the U.S. Army.

"The school-march, each day's festival": Title is taken from Ralph Waldo Emerson's poem "Threnody," found in *Selected Essays, Lectures, and Poems* (New York: Bantam Classics, 2007).

"Like a Blind Boy Jumping from Shed to Shed": The Stevie Wonder song referenced in the poem originally appeared on his 1969 album *My Cherie Amour* (Motown). Henry Crosby, Sylvia Moy, and Stevie Wonder composed the song.

"(So Tired of Standing Still We Got to) Move On": Title of the poem is the title of a James Brown song, which the artist composed and performed on his 1991 album *Love Over-due* (Scotti Bros. Records).

"Migratory Habits": Epigraph to the poem is from Robert Hayden's "A Plague of Starlings," found in *Collected Poems*, ed. Frederick Glaysher (New York: Liveright, 1985).

"Vertical Hold, 1967": Title of poem is taken from the title of a painting by Barkley L. Hendricks (American, b. 1945).

"Ne Me Quitte Pas": Title of the poem is the title of a song that Nina Simone performs on her *Live in Paris* album (Accord, 1996). Jacques Brel originally composed and recorded the song in 1958.

Acknowledgments

I owe debts, of gratitude and legal tender, which I cannot repay: to my teachers at Haverford College — C. Stephen Finley, Richard Freedman, Theresa Tensuan, and particularly to Raji Mohan and Gus Stadler, my first mentors — and Syracuse University — Michael Burkard, Arthur Flowers, Mary Karr, Chris Kennedy, Micere Githae Mugo, Bruce Smith, Silvio Torres-Saillant, and especially Brooks Haxton, for the rigorous but caring example he sets and for helping to shape these poems; to the fellows, faculty, and staff of Cave Canem, for their unconditional love and the gift of their poems; to Toi Derricotte and Cornelius Eady, for building us a house; to Emily Pulfer-Terino and Dilruba Ahmed, for thoughtful and thorough critiques that helped to improve some of these poems; to Chestnut Hill Academy and Syracuse University, specifically its African American Studies Department and Creative Writing Program, for providing financial support while I wrote these poems; to Krista Franklin, for her poems and her artistry and for allowing me to use her haunting collage on the cover; to Rachel Eliza Griffiths, for her gaze and the wonder of her poems; to Elizabeth Alexander, for pulling my manuscript out of the pile and for writing poems that empower us; to my friends from New Hartford, Clinton, Haverford, Boston, Syracuse, Cave Canem, and Philadelphia, for sustaining me with their intelligence, beauty, and love; to my in-laws Barry, Alison and Asher Feinberg, for accepting me into their family and supporting me with their love; to my sister Caitlin, for loving me even after growing up with me; to my parents Shelley Haley and Adrian Pollock, for their courage, for reading to me, for giving me *I am the Darker Brother*, and for their unstinting love; to Naomi, for more than I know how to say and for her love supreme — I write and live for you.

In addition, many thanks to the editors of the following publications, in which some poems originally appeared (sometimes in different versions):

AGNI (Online) ("Second Line")

Alehouse ("The Diaspora Remembers Guantánamo")

American Poetry Review Philadelphia Edition ("Hart Crane as Jim Crow"; "Shot & Killed")

Best New Poets 2010 ("*upon irremediable shores, those who never had time*")

Boston Review ("The Lieutenant, Returned")

Callaloo ("Queen of the Lower Ninth" as "Queen of the Ninth Ward"; "*Rattla cain't hold me*" as "All Your Sadness Will Be Arkansas")

Cimarron Review ("Snow in Wartime")

Crab Orchard Review ("Affection"; "*Ne Me Quitte Pas*" as "*Où L'amour Sera Roi*")

The Drunken Boat ("Child of the Sun"; "Like a Blind Boy Jumping from Shed to Shed")

Fourth River ("Flight" as "Instinct")

Harpur Palate ("Longing as Hoppin John")

Indiana Review ("*My Stove's in Good Condition*")

Poet Lore ("Beth David Cemetery, Long Island"; "The Recessive Gene")

Poetry Ink 2009 ("Medusa of Libya" as "Medusa")

Puerto del Sol ("On the Porch, Almost Men")

In particular, I thank the editors of *Callaloo* and *Crab Orchard Review* for their early support of my work.

CPSIA information can be obtained
at www.ICGtesting.com
Printed in the USA
LVHW020107090819
627063LV00001B/180/P